Published by Liberty Chidziwa at Createspace

1.0 EXECUTIVE SUMMARY

Bay 2 is a professional coffee bar shop and is determined to become a market leader in local coffee service to addicts. It will be a place to dream of as you try to escape the daily stresses of life and just a comfortable place to meet your friends or to read a book, all in one. It has free Wi-Fi internet to your favorite internet service providers. With the growing demand for high-quality gourmet coffee and great service, Bay 2 will capitalize on its proximity to the University of Michigan Campus to build a core group of repeat customers who are associated with our highly branded service. Bay 2 will offer its customers the best prepared coffee in the area that will be complimented with pastries, as well as free books that its patrons can read to enjoy their visit. The company will operate a 2,600 square foot coffee bar within a walking distance from the University of Michigan campus. The owners have secured this location from one of the directors own premise. They have also provided $140,000 of the required $170,000 start-up funds. The remaining capital will be obtained through Standard Chartered Bank.

The company is expected to grow sales revenue from $554,888 in 2014 to $706,000 in year three. As Bay 2 will strive to maintain a 66.5% gross profit margin and reasonable operating expenses, it will see net profits grow from $100,000 to $125,000 during the same period.

1.1 Objectives

The objectives for the first year of operations are:

- Become the leader in the Michigan area providing an excellent service second best to none.
- Make profits which sustain the business venture for the next three years
- Maintain a 65%-70 gross margin.

1.2 Key Success factors

The keys to success will be:

- Design a state of the art shop with a corporate identity that attract customers
- Employee high quality personal with a soft touch thereby providing a high quality service.
- Marketing strategies aimed to build a solid base of loyal customers, as well as maximizing the sales of high margin products, such as espresso drinks.

1.3 Mission

Bay 2 will make its best effort to create a unique service through our well trained staff .It aims at providing an service second best to none and make sure we maximize profits of the venture .Bay 2 will try to use an extensive marketing strategies of using promotions to attract customers .The payment option is going to be friendly and convenient. We will use cash and credit cards anf offer credit to our very loyal customers.

2.0 COMPANY SUMMARY.

2.1 Company Ownership

Bay 2 is a public limited liability company, sells coffee, other beverages and snacks in its 2,600 square feet premium coffee bar located near the University of Michigan campus. The two major investors are Tom Peters and Liberty Joe who cumulatively own over 70% of the company. The start-up loss of the company is assumed in the amount of $27,680

Bay 2 is registered as a Limited Liability Corporation in the state of Michigan. Tom Peters owns 51% of the company. His cousin, Liberty Joe, as well as Timothy Jackson and Jack Sue minority stakes in Bay 2, LLC.

2.2 Summary of start up expenses

The start-up expenses include:

- Legal expenses for obtaining licenses and permits as well as the accounting services totaling $1,300.
- Marketing promotion expenses for the grand opening of Bay 2 in the amount of $3,500 and as well as flyer printing (2,000 flyers at $0.04 per copy) for the total amount of $3,580.
- Consultants fees of $3,000 paid to Capricorn Accounting Business Consultants for the help with setting up the coffee bar.
- Insurance to Old Mutual (general liability, workers' compensation and property casualty) coverage at a total premium of $2,400.
- Pre-paid rent expenses for one month at $1.76 per square feet in the total amount of $4,576
- Premises remodeling in the amount of $9,824
- Other start-up expenses including stationery ($500) and phone and utility deposits ($2,500).

The required start-up assets of $142,320 include:

- Operating capital in the total amount of $67,123, which includes employees and owner's salaries of $23,900 for the first two months and cash reserves for the first three months of operation (approximately $14,400 per month).

- Start-up inventory of $16,027, which includes:

    - Coffee beans (12 regular brands and five decaffeinated brands) - $6,000
    - Coffee filters, baked goods, salads, sandwiches, tea, beverages, etc. - $7,900
    - Retail supplies (napkins, coffee bags, cleaning, etc.) - $1,840
    - Office supplies - $287
- Equipment for the total amount of $59,170:

    - Espresso machine - $6,000
    - Coffee maker - $900
    - Coffee grinder - $200
    - Food service equipment (microwave, toasters, dishwasher, refrigerator, blender, etc.) - $18,000
    - Storage hardware (bins, utensil rack, shelves, food case) - $3,720
    - Counter area equipment (counter top, sink, ice machine, etc.) - $9,500
    - Serving area equipment (plates, glasses, flatware) - $3,000
    - Store equipment (cash register, security, ventilation, signage) - $13,750
    - Office equipment (PC, fax/printer, phone, furniture, file cabinets) - $3,600
    - Other miscellaneous expenses - $500

Table: Start-up

Start-up	
Requirements	
Start-up Expenses	
Legal	$1,300
Stationery etc.	$500
Brochures	$3,580
Consultants	$3,000
Insurance	$2,400
Rent	$4,400
Remodeling	$10,000
Other	$2,500

Total Start-up Expenses	$27,680
Start-up Assets	
Cash Required	$67,123
Start-up Inventory	$16,027
Other Current Assets	$0
Long-term Assets	$59,170
Total Assets	$142,320
Total Requirements	$170,000

Table: Start-up Funding

Start-up Funding	
Start-up Expenses to Fund	$27,680
Start-up Assets to Fund	$142,320
Total Funding Required	$170,000
Assets	
Non-cash Assets from Start-up	$75,197
Cash Requirements from Start-up	$67,123
Additional Cash Raised	$0
Cash Balance on Starting Date	$67,123
Total Assets	$142,320
Liabilities and Capital	
Liabilities	
Current Borrowing	$10,000
Long-term Liabilities	$20,000
Accounts Payable (Outstanding Bills)	$0
Other Current Liabilities (interest-free)	$0
Total Liabilities	$30,000
Capital	
Planned Investment	
Tom Peters	$70,000
Liberty joe	$30,000
All other investors	$40,000
Additional Investment Requirement	$0
Total Planned Investment	$140,000
Loss at Start-up (Start-up Expenses)	($27,680)
Total Capital	$112,320
Total Capital and Liabilities	$142,320
Total Funding	$170,000

2.3 Physical evidence: Company address

Bay 2 Coffee bar will be located on the ground floor of the commercial building at the corner of West 13th Avenue and Patterson Street in Eugene, Michigan. The company has secured a one-year lease of the vacant 2,600 square feet premises previously occupied by car hire consultants. The lease contract has an option of renewal for five years at a fixed rate that Bay 2 will execute depending on the financial strength of its business.

The floor plan will include a 200 square feet back office and a 2,400 square feet coffee bar, which will include a seating area with 15 tables, a kitchen, storage area and two bathrooms. The space in the coffee bar will be approximately distributed the following way--1,360 square feet (i.e., 55% of the total) for the seating area, 600 square feet (26%) for the production area, and the remaining 440 square feet (19%) for the customer service area

This property is located in a commercial area within a walking distance from the University of Michigan campus on the corner of a major thoroughfare connecting affluent South Eugene neighborhood with the busy downtown commercial area. The commercially zoned premises have the necessary water and electricity hookups and will require only minor remodeling to accommodate the espresso bar, kitchen and storage area. The coffee bar's open and clean interior design with modern wooden decor will convey the quality of the served beverages and snacks, and will be in-line with the establishment's positioning as an eclectic place where people can relax and enjoy their cup of coffee. The clear window displays, through which passerby will be able to see customers enjoying their beverages, and outside electric signs will be aimed to grab the attention of the customer traffic.

3.0 SERVICE DESCRIPTION

Bay 2 will offer its customers the best tasting coffee beverages in the area. The service should be unique especially in efficiency and customer service delivery. This will be achieved by using high-quality ingredients and strictly following preparation guidelines. The store layout, menu listings and marketing activities will be focused on maximizing the sales of higher margin espresso drinks. High state of the art 72inch screens will be displaying the products outside the shop and inside. Along with the espresso drinks, brewed coffee and teas, as well as some refreshment beverages, will be sold in the coffee bar. Bay2 will also offer its clients pastries, small salads and sandwiches. For the gourmet clientele that prefers to prepare its coffee at home, Bay 2 will also be selling coffee beans. The menu offerings will be supplemented by free books and magazines that customers can read inside the coffee bar. For the most loyal customers internet token through Wi-Fi internet is going to be given so that customers take a longer time at the shop hence increasing purchases from repeated purchases.

3.1 Service Description

The menu of the Bay 2 coffee bar will be built around espresso-based coffee drinks such as lattes, mochas, cappuccinos, etc. Each of the espresso-based drinks will be offered with whole, skimmed, or soy milk. Each of these coffee beverages is based on a 'shot' of espresso, which is prepared in the espresso machine by forcing heated water through ground coffee at high pressure. Such espresso shots are combined with steamed milk and/or other additives like cocoa, caramel, etc., to prepare the espresso-based beverages. Proper preparation techniques are of paramount importance for such drinks. A minor deviation from the amount of coffee in the shot, the size of the coffee particles, the temperature of milk, etc., can negatively affect the quality of the prepared drink.

3.2 Sales Literature

Our sales literature is going to be made by Gontac Graphic designers with our corporate color brown colour.The company logo is going to have a cup of coffee smoldering with hot smoke showing hot coffee. The designers are going to work with Mr. Liberty Joe who has the experience in Graphic designing. The 2,000 flyers are going to be disturbed a week just prior to opening in the Michigan Shopping Complex Mall.

4.0 MARKET SEGMENT

4.1 Market research

According to the research in Coffee beverages by Capitec Market Research Consultants, the U.S. coffee consumption has shown steady growth, with gourmet coffee having the strongest growth. Coffee drinkers in the Pacific Northwest are among the most demanding ones. They favor well-brewed gourmet coffee drinks and demand great service. Eugene, OR, with its liberal and outgoing populace and long rainy winter, has traditionally been a great place for coffee establishments. Bay 2 will strive to build a loyal customer base by offering a great tasting coffee in a relaxing environment of its coffee bar located close to the bustling University of Michigan Campus. This is a potential market for students.

4.2 Market Segmentation

Bay 2 will focus its marketing activities on reaching the University students and faculty, people working in offices located close to the coffee bar and on sophisticated teenagers. Our market research shows that these are the customer groups that are most likely to buy gourmet coffee products. Since gourmet coffee consumption is universal across different income categories and mostly depends on the level of higher education, proximity to the University of Michigan campus will provide access to the targeted customer audience.

4.3 Table: Market Analysis

Market Analysis							
		Year 1	Year 2	Year 3	Year 4	Year 5	
Potential Customers	Growth						CAGR
Students and Faculty	2%	18,000	18,360	18,727	19,102	19,484	2.00%
Teenagers	1%	3,000	3,030	3,060	3,091	3,122	1.00%
Office workers	2%	8,000	8,160	8,323	8,489	8,659	2.00%
Other	0%	5,000	5,000	5,000	5,000	5,000	0.00%
Total	1.63%	34,000	34,550	35,110	35,682	36,265	1.63%

4.5 Target Market Segment Strategy

Bay 2 will cater to people who want to get their daily cup of great-tasting coffee in a relaxing atmosphere. Such customers vary in age, although our location close to the University campus means that most of our clientele will be college students and faculty. Our market research shows that these are discerning customers that gravitate towards better tasting coffee. Furthermore, a lot of college students consider coffee bars to be a convenient studying or meeting location, where they can read or meet with peers without the necessity to pay cover charges. Sometimes, it is also the area for the internet surfers use our free Wi-Fi when they are loyal, especially those students who want a quiet environment .For us, this will provide a unique possibility for building a loyal client base.

4.5.1 Market Needs

General trend toward quality among U.S. consumers definitely plays an important role in the recent growth in gourmet coffee. Additionally, such factors as desire for small indulgencies, for something more exotic and unique, provide a good selling opportunity for coffee bars. Coffee is well known for the caffeine which help to reduce stress and increase concentration of the mind.

4.6 Industry Analysis

Coffee consumption has shown a steady 4.5% growth rate in the United States over the last decade. In 2014, total sales of coffee were approximately $7.5 billion with gourmet coffee representing 33% (or $2.5 billion) of that. The retail coffee industry is flourishing in the U.S. Pacific Northwest and most regions. The local climate, with a long rainy season, is very conducive for the consumption of hot non-alcoholic beverages. At the same time, hot dry summers drive people into cafes to order iced drinks. Further, coffee has really become a part of the lifestyle in the Pacific Northwest. Its discerning coffee drinkers are in favor of well-prepared, strong coffee-based beverages, which they can consume in a relaxing environment.

4.6.1 Competition and Buying Patterns

Competition analysis

According to the 2014 Michigan Food service Statistics , Liberty Joe had 45 established snack & non-alcoholic beverage bar with total sales of $14.2 million. Among other establishments that offer coffee drinks to their customers are most of Liberty's limited- and full-service restaurants. Bay 2's direct competitors will be other coffee bars located near the University of Michigan campus. These include Starbucks, Cafe Roma, The UO Bookstore, and other Food service establishments that offer coffee. Starbucks will definitely be one of the major competitors because of its strong financial position and established marketing and operational practices. However, despite of Starbuck's entrenched market position, many customers favor smaller, independent establishments that offer cozy atmosphere and good coffee at affordable prices. Cafe Roma is a good example of such competition. We estimate that Starbucks holds approximately 35% market share in that neighborhood, Cafe Roma appeals to 25% of customers, The UO Bookstore caters to another 10%, with the remaining market share split among other establishments. Bay 2 will position itself as a unique coffee bar that not only offers the best tasting coffee and pastries but also provides home-like, cozy and comfortable environment, which established corporate establishments lack. We will cater to customers' bodies and minds, which will help us grow our market share in this competitive market.

Buying Patterns

The major reason for the customers to return to a specific coffee bar is a great tasting coffee, quick service and pleasant atmosphere. Although, as stated before, coffee consumption is uniform across different income segments, Bay 2 will price its product offerings competitively. We strongly believe that selling coffee with a great service in a nice setting will help us build a strong base of loyal clientele.

5.0 STRATEGIC IMPLEMENTATION SEGMENT

Bay 2 Cultures marketing strategy will be focused at getting new customers, retaining the existing customers, getting customers to spend more and come back more often. Establishing a loyal customer base is of a paramount importance since such customer core will not only generate most of the sales but also will provide favorable referrals.

5.1 Competitive analysis

Bay 2 will position itself as unique coffee bar where its patrons can not only enjoy a cup of perfectly brewed coffee but also spend their time in an ambient environment. Comfortable sofas and chairs, dimmed light and quiet relaxing music will help the customers to relax from the daily stresses and will differentiate Bay 2 from incumbent competitors.

5.2 Sales Strategy

Bay 2 baristas will handle the sales transactions. To speed up the customer service, at least two employees will be servicing clients--while one employee will be preparing the customer's order, the other one will be taking care of the sales transaction. All sales data logged on the computerized point-of-sale terminal will be later analyzed for marketing purposes. In order to build up its client base, Bay 2 will use banners and fliers, utilize customer referrals and cross-promotions with other businesses in the community. At the same time, customer retention programs will be used to make sure the customers are coming back and spending more at the coffee bar.

5.2.1 Sales Forecast

Food costs are assumed at 25% for coffee beverages and 50% for retail beans and pastries. Proximity to the University campus will dictate certain sales seasonality with revenues slightly decreasing during the school vacation periods.

Table: Sales Forecast

Sales Forecast	Year 1	Year 2	Year 3
Sales			
Coffee beverages	$350,400	$385,440	$423,984
Coffee beans	$87,600	$96,360	$105,996
Pastries, etc.	$146,000	$160,600	$176,660
Total Sales	$584,000	$642,400	$706,640
Direct Cost of Sales	Year 1	Year 2	Year 3
Coffee beverages	$87,600	$96,360	$105,996
Coffee beans	$43,800	$48,180	$52,998
Pastries, etc.	$73,000	$80,300	$88,330
Subtotal Direct Cost of Sales	$204,400	$224,840	$247,324

6.0 MANAGEMENT SEGMENT

Bay 2 is majority-owned by Tom Peters and Liberty Joe holds a Bachelor's Degree in Business Studies from the University of Cape Pensula in South Africa (Cape Town). He's worked for several years as an independent business consultant. Previously, he owned the ABC Travel Agency and Capitec Group of Companies, the later which he profitably sold four years ago. Mr. Tom Peters has extensive business contacts in Michigan that he will leverage to help his new venture succeed. Mr. Joe has a Bachelor's Degree in Tourism and Hospitality from the Don Bosco State University. Currently, he is doing a Mcom in Strategic Management with Boston University. For the last five years he has worked as a manager of DEF Ristorante, a successful Italian restaurant in Kansas. Under Mr. Joe's management, the restaurant has consistently increased sales while maintaining a lower than average level of operating expenses. He has a keen passion in service marketing

However, because of the investors' other commitments they will not be involved into the daily management decisions at Bay 2. A professional manager ($35,000/yr) will be hired who will oversee all the coffee bar operations. The manager must have at least 5 years experience in tourism possibly with a catering degree or a post graduate diploma in tourism. Two full-time baristas ($25,000/yr each) will be in charge of coffee preparation. These should be well qualified personnel with at least 2 years in the hotel or coffee preparation job .Four more part-time employees will be hired to fulfill the staffing needs. In the second and third year of operation one more part-time employee will be hired to handle the increased sales volume. We are also collaborating with The University of Michigan for 2 internship students or for attachments as part of our social responsibility programme.

6.1 Management Team

A full-time manager will be hired to oversee the daily operations at Bay 2. The candidate (whose name is withheld due to his current employment commitment) has had five years of managerial experience in the definitely industry in Michigan. This person's responsibilities will include managing the staff, ordering inventory, dealing with suppliers, developing a marketing strategy and perform other daily managerial duties. We believe that our candidate has the right experience for this role. A profit-sharing arrangement for the manager may be considered based on the first year operational results.

6.2 Management Consultants

Despite the owners' and manager's experience in the definitely industry, the company will retain the consulting services of Grantsock Espresso Services, the consultants who have helped to develop the business idea for Bay 2. This company has over twenty years of experience in the retail coffee industry and has successfully opened dozens of coffee bars across the U.S. Consultants will be primarily used for market research, customer satisfaction surveys and to provide additional input into the evaluation of the new business opportunities.

6.3 Personnel Plan

The table below outlines the personnel needs of Bay2.

Table: Personnel

Personnel Plan	Year 1	Year 2	Year 3
Manager	$35,000	$37,800	$40,824
Baristas	$50,000	$54,000	$58,320
Employees	$39,600	$52,000	$56,000
Total People	7	8	8
Total Payroll	$124,600	$143,800	$155,144

7.0 FINANCIAL PLAN SEGMENT

Bay 2 will capitalize on the strong demand for high-quality gourmet coffee. The owners have provided the company with sufficient start-up capital. With successful management aimed at establishing and growing a loyal customer base, the company will see its net worth doubling in two years. Bay2 will maintain a healthy 66.5% gross margin, which combined with reasonable operating expenses, will provide enough cash to finance further growth.

7.1 Important Assumptions

Table: General Assumptions

General Assumptions			
	Year 1	Year 2	Year 3
Plan Month	1	2	3
Current Interest Rate	10.00%	10.00%	10.00%
Long-term Interest Rate	10.00%	10.00%	10.00%
Tax Rate	25.42%	25.00%	25.42%
Other	0	0	0

7.2 Cash Flow forecasts

As the chart and table below present, the company will maintain a healthy cash flow position, which will allow for timely debt servicing and funds available for future development.

Chart: Cash

Cash Flow Projections

Projected Cash Flows			
	Year 1	Year 2	Year 3
Cash Received			
Cash from Operations			
Cash Sales	$584,000	$642,400	$706,640
Subtotal Cash from Operations	$584,000	$642,400	$706,640
Additional Cash Received			
VAT,	$0	$0	$0
New Current Borrowing	$0	$0	$0
New Other Liabilities (interest-free)	$0	$0	$0
New Long-term Liabilities	$0	$0	$0
Sales of Other Current Assets	$0	$0	$0
Sales of Long-term Assets	$0	$0	$0
New Investment Received	$0	$0	$0
Subtotal Cash Received	$584,000	$642,400	$706,640
Expenditures	Year 1	Year 2	Year 3
Expenditures from Operations			
Cash Spending	$124,600	$143,800	$155,144
Bill Payments	$327,865	$388,144	$420,837
Subtotal Spent on Operations	$452,465	$531,944	$575,981
Additional Cash Spent			
Sales Tax, VAT	$0	$0	$0
Principal Repayment of Current Borrowing	$3,300	$3,300	$3,300
Other Liabilities Principal Repayment	$0	$0	$0
Long-term Liabilities Principal Repayment	$0	$3,585	$3,961
Purchase Other Current Assets	$0	$0	$0
Purchase Long-term Assets	$0	$2,000	$2,000
Dividends	$0	$0	$0

Subtotal Cash Spent	$455,765	$540,829	$585,242
Net Cash Flow	$128,235	$101,571	$121,398
Cash Balance	$195,358	$296,928	$418,326

7.3 Break-even Analysis

With average monthly fixed costs of $20,300 in FY2014 and an average margin of 65%, Bay 2 break-even sales volume is around $31,300 per month. As shown further, the company is expected to generate such sales volume from the outstart.

Table: Break-even Analysis

Break-even Analysis	
Monthly Revenue Break-even	$31,247
Assumptions:	
Average Percent Variable Cost	35%
Estimated Monthly Fixed Cost	$20,311

7.5 Projected Income statements (Profit and loss)

Annual projected sales of $584,000 in FY2014 translate into $254.00 of sales per square foot, which is in line with the industry averages for this size of coffee bar. Overall, as the company gets established in the local market, its net profitability increases from 17.06% in FY2014 to 17.63% in FY2016. The table below outlines the projected Profit and Loss Statement for FY2014-2016.

Projected income statements for the 3 years			
	Year 1	Year 2	Year 3
Sales	$584,000	$642,400	$706,640
Direct Cost of Sales	$204,400	$224,840	$247,324
Other	$0	$0	$0
Total Cost of Sales	$204,400	$224,840	$247,324
Gross Margin	$379,600	$417,560	$459,316
Gross Margin %	66.5.00%	66.00%	68.00%
Expenses			
Payroll	$124,600	$143,800	$155,144
Sales and Marketing and Other Expenses	$25,800	$27,600	$31,000
Depreciation	$5,400	$5,500	$5,500
Rent	$48,400	$52,800	$52,800
Rent	$6,000	$6,000	$6,000
Maintenance	$5,840	$6,424	$7,066
Utilities/Phone	$9,000	$9,500	$10,000
Payroll Taxes	$18,690	$21,570	$23,272
Other	$0	$0	$0
Total Operating Expenses	$243,730	$273,194	$290,782
Profit Before Interest and Taxes	$135,870	$144,366	$168,534
EBITDA	$141,270	$149,866	$174,034
Interest Expense	$2,821	$2,326	$1,618
Taxes Incurred	$33,740	$35,510	$42,424
Net Profit	$99,308	$106,530	$124,491
Net Profit/Sales	17.00%	16.58%	17.62%

7.6 Projected Balance Sheet

The company's net worth is expected to increase from approximately $212,000 by the end of FY2014 to approximately $443,000 in FY2016. The table below summarizes the projected balance sheets for this period.

Pro Forma Balance Sheet	Year 1	Year 2	Year 3
Assets			
Current Assets			
Cash	$195,358	$296,928	$418,326
Inventory	$21,175	$22,671	$24,939
Other Current Assets	$0	$0	$0
Total Current Assets	$216,533	$319,600	$443,264
Long-term Assets			
Long-term Assets	$59,170	$61,170	$63,170
Accumulated Depreciation	$5,400	$10,900	$16,400
Total Long-term Assets	$53,770	$50,270	$46,770
Total Assets	$270,303	$369,870	$490,034
Liabilities and Capital	Year 1	Year 2	Year 3
Current Liabilities			
Accounts Payable	$31,974	$31,896	$34,831
Current Borrowing	$6,700	$3,400	$100
Other Current Liabilities	$0	$0	$0
Subtotal Current Liabilities	$38,674	$35,296	$34,931
Long-term Liabilities	$20,000	$16,415	$12,454
Total Liabilities	$58,674	$51,711	$47,385
Paid-in Capital	$140,000	$140,000	$140,000
Retained Earnings	($27,680)	$71,628	$178,159
Earnings	$99,308	$106,530	$124,491
Total Capital	$211,628	$318,159	$442,650
Total Liabilities and Capital	$270,303	$369,870	$490,034

Net Worth	$211,628	$318,159	$442,650

7.7 Ratio Analysis

Table: Ratios

	Year 1	Year 2	Year 3	Industry Profile
Sales Growth	n.a.	10.00%	10.00%	7.60%
Percent of Total Assets				
Inventory	7.83%	6.13%	5.09%	3.60%
Other Current Assets	0.00%	0.00%	0.00%	35.60%
Total Current Assets	80.11%	86.41%	90.46%	43.70%
Long-term Assets	19.89%	13.59%	9.54%	56.30%
Total Assets	100.00%	100.00%	100.00%	100.00%
Current Liabilities	14.31%	9.54%	7.13%	32.70%
Long-term Liabilities	7.40%	4.44%	2.54%	28.50%
Total Liabilities	21.71%	13.98%	9.67%	61.20%
Net Worth	78.29%	86.02%	90.33%	38.80%
Percent of Sales				
Sales	100.00%	100.00%	100.00%	100.00%
Gross Margin	65.00%	65.00%	65.00%	60.50%
Selling, General & Administrative Expenses	47.94%	48.47%	47.37%	39.80%
Advertising Expenses	2.26%	2.18%	2.26%	3.20%
Profit Before Interest and Taxes	23.27%	22.47%	23.85%	0.70%
Main Ratios				
Current	5.60	9.05	12.69	0.98
Quick	5.05	8.41	11.98	0.65
Total Debt to Total Assets	21.71%	13.98%	9.67%	61.20%
Pre-tax Return on Net Worth	62.87%	44.64%	37.71%	1.70%
Pre-tax Return on Assets	49.22%	38.40%	34.06%	4.30%
Additional Ratios	Year 1	Year 2	Year 3	
Net Profit Margin	17.00%	16.58%	17.62%	n.a
Return on Equity	46.93%	33.48%	28.12%	n.a

Activity Ratios				
Inventory Turnover	10.91	10.26	10.39	n.a
Accounts Payable Turnover	11.25	12.17	12.17	n.a
Payment Days	27	30	29	n.a
Total Asset Turnover	2.16	1.74	1.44	n.a
Debt Ratios				
Debt to Net Worth	0.28	0.16	0.11	n.a
Current Liab. to Liab.	0.66	0.68	0.74	n.a
Liquidity Ratios				
Net Working Capital	$177,858	$284,304	$408,334	n.a
Interest Coverage	48.16	62.07	104.13	n.a
Additional Ratios				
Assets to Sales	0.46	0.58	0.69	n.a
Current Debt/Total Assets	14%	10%	7%	n.a
Acid Test	5.05	8.41	11.98	n.a
Sales/Net Worth	2.76	2.02	1.60	n.a
Dividend Payout	0.00	0.00	0.00	n.a

Table: Sales Forecast

Sales Forecast		Month 1	Month 2	Month 3	Month 4	Month 5	Month 6	Month 7	Month 8	Month 9	Month 10	Month 11	Month 12
Sales													
Coffee beverages	0%	$24,000	$27,000	$28,800	$28,800	$28,800	$28,800	$28,800	$28,800	$29,400	$31,200	$33,000	$33,000
Coffee beans	0%	$6,000	$6,750	$7,200	$7,200	$7,200	$7,200	$7,200	$7,200	$7,350	$7,800	$8,250	$8,250
Pastries, etc.	0%	$10,000	$11,250	$12,000	$12,000	$12,000	$12,000	$12,000	$12,000	$12,250	$13,000	$13,750	$13,750
Total Sales		$40,000	$45,000	$48,000	$48,000	$48,000	$48,000	$48,000	$48,000	$49,000	$52,000	$55,000	$55,000
Direct Cost of Sales		Month 1	Month 2	Month 3	Month 4	Month 5	Month 6	Month 7	Month 8	Month 9	Month 10	Month 11	Month 12
Coffee beverages		$6,000	$6,750	$7,200	$7,200	$7,200	$7,200	$7,200	$7,200	$7,350	$7,800	$8,250	$8,250
Coffee beans		$3,000	$3,375	$3,600	$3,600	$3,600	$3,600	$3,600	$3,600	$3,675	$3,900	$4,125	$4,125
Pastries, etc.		$5,000	$5,625	$6,000	$6,000	$6,000	$6,000	$6,000	$6,000	$6,125	$6,500	$6,875	$6,875
Subtotal Direct Cost of Sales		$14,000	$15,750	$16,800	$16,800	$16,800	$16,800	$16,800	$16,800	$17,150	$18,200	$19,250	$19,250

Table: Personnel

Personnel Plan		Month 1	Month 2	Month 3	Month 4	Month 5	Month 6	Month 7	Month 8	Month 9	Month 10	Month 11	Month 12
Manager	0 %	$2,917	$2,917	$2,917	$2,917	$2,917	$2,917	$2,917	$2,917	$2,917	$2,917	$2,917	$2,917
Baristas	0 %	$4,167	$4,167	$4,167	$4,167	$4,167	$4,167	$4,167	$4,167	$4,167	$4,167	$4,167	$4,167
Employees	0 %	$3,300	$3,300	$3,300	$3,300	$3,300	$3,300	$3,300	$3,300	$3,300	$3,300	$3,300	$3,300
Total People		7	7	7	7	7	7	7	7	7	7	7	7
Total Payroll		$10,383	$10,383	$10,383	$10,383	$10,383	$10,383	$10,383	$10,383	$10,383	$10,383	$10,383	$10,383

Table: General Assumptions

General Assumptions	Month 1	Month 2	Month 3	Month 4	Month 5	Month 6	Month 7	Month 8	Month 9	Month 10	Month 11	Month 12
Plan Month	1	2	3	4	5	6	7	8	9	10	11	12
Current Interest Rate	10.00%	10.00%	10.00%	10.00%	10.00%	10.00%	10.00%	10.00%	10.00%	10.00%	10.00%	10.00%
Long-term Interest Rate	10.00%	10.00%	10.00%	10.00%	10.00%	10.00%	10.00%	10.00%	10.00%	10.00%	10.00%	10.00%
Tax Rate	30.00%	25.00%	25.00%	25.00%	25.00%	25.00%	25.00%	25.00%	25.00%	25.00%	25.00%	25.00%
Other	0	0	0	0	0	0	0	0	0	0	0	0

Table: Profit and Loss

Pro Forma Profit and Loss		Month 1	Month 2	Month 3	Month 4	Month 5	Month 6	Month 7	Month 8	Month 9	Month 10	Month 11	Month 12
Sales		$40,000	$45,000	$48,000	$48,000	$48,000	$48,000	$48,000	$48,000	$49,000	$52,000	$55,000	$55,000
Direct Cost of Sales		$14,000	$15,750	$16,800	$16,800	$16,800	$16,800	$16,800	$16,800	$17,150	$18,200	$19,250	$19,250
Other		$0	$0	$0	$0	$0	$0	$0	$0	$0	$0	$0	$0
Total Cost of Sales		$14,000	$15,750	$16,800	$16,800	$16,800	$16,800	$16,800	$16,800	$17,150	$18,200	$19,250	$19,250
Gross Margin		$26,000	$29,250	$31,200	$31,200	$31,200	$31,200	$31,200	$31,200	$31,850	$33,800	$35,750	$35,750
Gross Margin %		65.00%	65.00%	65.00%	65.00%	65.00%	65.00%	65.00%	65.00%	65.00%	65.00%	65.00%	65.00%
Expenses													
Payroll		$10,383	$10,383	$10,383	$10,383	$10,383	$10,383	$10,383	$10,383	$10,383	$10,383	$10,383	$10,383
Sales and Marketing and Other Expenses		$2,150	$2,150	$2,150	$2,150	$2,150	$2,150	$2,150	$2,150	$2,150	$2,150	$2,150	$2,150
Depreciation		$450	$450	$450	$450	$450	$450	$450	$450	$450	$450	$450	$450
Rent		$0	$4,400	$4,400	$4,400	$4,400	$4,400	$4,400	$4,400	$4,400	$4,400	$4,400	$4,400
Rent		$500	$500	$500	$500	$500	$500	$500	$500	$500	$500	$500	$500
Maintenance		$400	$450	$480	$480	$480	$480	$480	$480	$490	$520	$550	$550
Utilities/Phone		$750	$750	$750	$750	$750	$750	$750	$750	$750	$750	$750	$750
Payroll Taxes	15%	$1,558	$1,558	$1,558	$1,558	$1,558	$1,558	$1,558	$1,558	$1,558	$1,558	$1,558	$1,558
Other		$0	$0	$0	$0	$0	$0	$0	$0	$0	$0	$0	$0
Total Operating Expenses		$16,191	$20,641	$20,671	$20,671	$20,671	$20,671	$20,671	$20,671	$20,681	$20,711	$20,741	$20,741
Profit Before Interest and Taxes		$9,809	$8,609	$10,529	$10,529	$10,529	$10,529	$10,529	$10,529	$11,169	$13,089	$15,009	$15,009
EBITDA		$10,259	$9,059	$10,979	$10,979	$10,979	$10,979	$10,979	$10,979	$11,619	$13,539	$15,459	$15,459
Interest Expense		$248	$245	$243	$241	$239	$236	$234	$232	$229	$227	$225	$223
Taxes		$2,868	$2,091	$2,572	$2,572	$2,573	$2,573	$2,574	$2,574	$2,735	$3,216	$3,696	$3,697

Incurred

Net Profit	.	$6,693	$6,273	$7,715	$7,716	$7,718	$7,720	$7,721	$7,723	$8,205	$9,647	$11,088	$11,090
Net Profit/Sales		16.73%	13.94%	16.07%	16.08%	16.08%	16.08%	16.09%	16.09%	16.74%	18.55%	20.16%	20.16%

Table: Cash Flow

Pro Forma Cash Flow		Month 1	Month 2	Month 3	Month 4	Month 5	Month 6	Month 7	Month 8	Month 9	Month 10	Month 11	Month 12
Cash Received													
Cash from Operations													
Cash Sales		$40,000	$45,000	$48,000	$48,000	$48,000	$48,000	$48,000	$48,000	$49,000	$52,000	$55,000	$55,000
Subtotal Cash from Operations		$40,000	$45,000	$48,000	$48,000	$48,000	$48,000	$48,000	$48,000	$49,000	$52,000	$55,000	$55,000
Additional Cash Received													
Sales Tax, VAT, HST/GST Received	0.00%	$0	$0	$0	$0	$0	$0	$0	$0	$0	$0	$0	$0
New Current Borrowing		$0	$0	$0	$0	$0	$0	$0	$0	$0	$0	$0	$0
New Other Liabilities (interest-free)		$0	$0	$0	$0	$0	$0	$0	$0	$0	$0	$0	$0
New Long-term Liabilities		$0	$0	$0	$0	$0	$0	$0	$0	$0	$0	$0	$0
Sales of Other Current Assets		$0	$0	$0	$0	$0	$0	$0	$0	$0	$0	$0	$0
Sales of Long-term Assets		$0	$0	$0	$0	$0	$0	$0	$0	$0	$0	$0	$0
New Investment Received		$0	$0	$0	$0	$0	$0	$0	$0	$0	$0	$0	$0
Subtotal Cash Received		$40,000	$45,000	$48,000	$48,000	$48,000	$48,000	$48,000	$48,000	$49,000	$52,000	$55,000	$55,000

Expenditures		Month 1	Month 2	Month 3	Month 4	Month 5	Month 6	Month 7	Month 8	Month 9	Month 10	Month 11	Month 12
Expenditures from Operations													
Cash Spending		$10,383	$10,383	$10,383	$10,383	$10,383	$10,383	$10,383	$10,383	$10,383	$10,383	$10,383	$10,383
Bill Payments		$728	$22,112	$29,845	$30,569	$29,450	$29,449	$29,447	$29,445	$29,474	$30,424	$32,727	$34,195
Subtotal Spent on Operations		$11,112	$32,496	$40,228	$40,952	$39,834	$39,832	$39,830	$39,829	$39,857	$40,808	$43,110	$44,578
Additional Cash Spent													
Sales Tax, VAT, HST/GST Paid Out		$0	$0	$0	$0	$0	$0	$0	$0	$0	$0	$0	$0
Principal Repayment of Current Borrowing		$275	$275	$275	$275	$275	$275	$275	$275	$275	$275	$275	$275
Other Liabilities Principal Repayment		$0	$0	$0	$0	$0	$0	$0	$0	$0	$0	$0	$0
Long-term Liabilities Principal Repayment		$0	$0	$0	$0	$0	$0	$0	$0	$0	$0	$0	$0
Purchase Other Current Assets		$0	$0	$0	$0	$0	$0	$0	$0	$0	$0	$0	$0
Purchase Long-term Assets		$0	$0	$0	$0	$0	$0	$0	$0	$0	$0	$0	$0
Dividends		$0	$0	$0	$0	$0	$0	$0	$0	$0	$0	$0	$0
Subtotal Cash Spent		$11,387	$32,771	$40,503	$41,227	$40,109	$40,107	$40,105	$40,104	$40,132	$41,083	$43,385	$44,853
Net Cash Flow		$28,613	$12,229	$7,497	$6,773	$7,891	$7,893	$7,895	$7,896	$8,868	$10,917	$11,615	$10,147

		Month 1	Month 2	Month 3	Month 4	Month 5	Month 6	Month 7	Month 8	Month 9	Month 10	Month 11	Month 12
Cash Balance		$95,736	$107,966	$115,462	$122,235	$130,127	$138,020	$145,914	$153,811	$162,679	$173,596	$185,211	$195,358

Table: Balance Sheet

Pro Forma Balance Sheet													
Assets	Starting Balances	Month 1	Month 2	Month 3	Month 4	Month 5	Month 6	Month 7	Month 8	Month 9	Month 10	Month 11	Month 12
Current Assets													
Cash	$67,123	$95,736	$107,966	$115,462	$122,235	$130,127	$138,020	$145,914	$153,811	$162,679	$173,596	$185,211	$195,358
Inventory	$16,027	$15,400	$17,325	$18,480	$18,480	$18,480	$18,480	$18,480	$18,480	$18,865	$20,020	$21,175	$21,175
Other Current Assets	$0	$0	$0	$0	$0	$0	$0	$0	$0	$0	$0	$0	$0
Total Current Assets	$83,150	$111,136	$125,291	$133,942	$140,715	$148,607	$156,500	$164,394	$172,291	$181,544	$193,616	$206,386	$216,533
Long-term Assets													
Long-term Assets	$59,170	$59,170	$59,170	$59,170	$59,170	$59,170	$59,170	$59,170	$59,170	$59,170	$59,170	$59,170	$59,170
Accumulated Depreciation	$0	$450	$900	$1,350	$1,800	$2,250	$2,700	$3,150	$3,600	$4,050	$4,500	$4,950	$5,400
Total Long-term Assets	$59,170	$58,720	$58,270	$57,820	$57,370	$56,920	$56,470	$56,020	$55,570	$55,120	$54,670	$54,220	$53,770
Total Assets	$142,320	$169,856	$183,561	$191,762	$198,085	$205,527	$212,970	$220,414	$227,861	$236,664	$248,286	$260,606	$270,303
Liabilities and Capital		Month 1	Month 2	Month 3	Month 4	Month 5	Month 6	Month 7	Month 8	Month 9	Month 10	Month 11	Month 12
Current Liabilities													

Accounts Payable	$0	$21,118	$28,825	$29,587	$28,469	$28,467	$28,465	$28,464	$28,462	$29,335	$31,586	$33,092	$31,974
Current Borrowing	$10,000	$9,725	$9,450	$9,175	$8,900	$8,625	$8,350	$8,075	$7,800	$7,525	$7,250	$6,975	$6,700
Other Current Liabilities	$0	$0	$0	$0	$0	$0	$0	$0	$0	$0	$0	$0	$0
Subtotal Current Liabilities	$10,000	$30,843	$38,275	$38,762	$37,369	$37,092	$36,815	$36,539	$36,262	$36,860	$38,836	$40,067	$38,674
Long-term Liabilities	$20,000	$20,000	$20,000	$20,000	$20,000	$20,000	$20,000	$20,000	$20,000	$20,000	$20,000	$20,000	$20,000
Total Liabilities	$30,000	$50,843	$58,275	$58,762	$57,369	$57,092	$56,815	$56,539	$56,262	$56,860	$58,836	$60,067	$58,674
Paid-in Capital	$140,000	$140,000	$140,000	$140,000	$140,000	$140,000	$140,000	$140,000	$140,000	$140,000	$140,000	$140,000	$140,000
Retained Earnings	($27,680)	($27,680)	($27,680)	($27,680)	($27,680)	($27,680)	($27,680)	($27,680)	($27,680)	($27,680)	($27,680)	($27,680)	($27,680)
Earnings	$0	$6,693	$12,966	$20,680	$28,397	$36,115	$43,834	$51,559	$59,274	$67,480	$77,130	$88,218	$99,308
Total Capital	$112,320	$119,013	$125,286	$133,000	$140,717	$148,435	$156,154	$163,876	$171,599	$179,804	$189,450	$200,538	$211,628
Total Liabilities and Capital	$142,320	$169,856	$183,561	$191,762	$198,085	$205,527	$212,970	$220,414	$227,861	$236,664	$248,286	$260,606	$270,303
Net Worth	$112,320	$119,013	$125,286	$133,000	$140,717	$148,435	$156,154	$163,876	$171,599	$179,804	$189,450	$200,538	$211,628

Thank you for reading my book. If you have enjoyed it, won't leave me a review at your favourite retailer?

Thanks

Liberty Chidziwa

About the Author:

Liberty Chidziwa is business analyst, consultant in accounting, payroll and a marketing research consultant. He holds an Honours degree in marketing and business Studies. Currently, he is studying towards an MBA in project management to master his entrepreneurial flair. He is running Capricorn Consultants Pty in South Africa, a branch of Ree and Lee Accounting Business Consultants which was operating in Ondangwa Namibia. He is also the owner of Grantsock Investments in 100% ownership which is a secretarial accounting registration company. The author has a passion for entrepreneurial vision and helps much in small start up advice.

Expert more books to come soon in the following topics

Title 1: Business Plans for Entrepreneurs:(Various Business plans)

Title 2: Branded for greatness

Title 3: Research proposal secrets

Title 4: Mafia marketing

Connect with me on LinkedIn, Twitter and Face book,

CreateSpace eStore: https://www.createspace.com/4936179

Email address:libchid@gmail.com

Phone +27730906169,   Whatsapp +27730906169